Many wild animals eat in one place and shelter in another place. WomWom wants to explore!

Some animals live in the same area as WomWom. They do not shelter in the same place as WomWom! What are the places where animals live?

WomWom eats grass over a big area. WomWom shelters in a small place called her burrow. She goes into her burrow to shelter when she is not eating.

Earthworms live in the
compost and in soil.
WomWom looks at the
earthworms in the compost.

Some animals do not live in a burrow like WomWom. Possums live in trees. The possum is safe from danger.

WomWom hides in her burrow. WomWom hides from danger. What do other animals do when there is danger? A young kangaroo hides in its mother's pouch.

Birds make a nest for shelter
and to hatch their eggs. Birds
can make nests in trees, in
burrows or on the ground.

WomWom can see the kookaburras sitting in the tree for shelter. The leaves give them shade from the sun.

Many animals live close to each other. WomWom often visits the hens. The hens and WomWom also take shelter in different places.

WomWom knows that her friends in the ocean are different from animals on the land. The dolphins do not have a nest or a burrow. Dolphins swim together in a group. A group of dolphins is called a pod.

Young wombats with no mothers live together at a carer's house. The carer feeds them milk and gives them shelter.

What can WomWom do if
there is no fresh grass to eat
near her burrow? She can
use her strong legs to walk to
another area. She can dig a
new burrow where there is
fresh grass close by.